FLAMMABLE MATTER

FLAMMABLE MATTER

JACOB VICTORINE

ELIXIR PRESS | DENVER, COLORADO

FLAMMABLE MATTER. Copyright © 2016 by Jacob Victorine. All rights reserved. Printed in the United States of America. For information, address Elixir Press, PO Box 27029, Denver, CO 80227.

www.elixirpress.com

Cover art by Jim Victorine and inspired by Manish Swarup's photo of Jamphel Yeshi for the AP
Book design by Steven Seighman

Library of Congress Cataloging-in-Publication Data
Victorine, Jacob.
[Poems. Selections]
Flammable matter / Jacob Victorine.
   pages cm
Includes bibliographical references.
Summary: "Winner of the Elixir Press Poetry Awards."
ISBN 978-1-932418-59-0 (alk. paper)
I. Title.
PS3622.I2889A6 2016 811'.6—dc23
                                                      2015029474

10 9 8 7 6 5 4 3 2 1

For Kyi, Malachi, Zarmina,
and too many others

Contents

Set Fire to Yourself or Don't	1
Flammable Matter	2
Morocco	3
Sherab Tsedor	4
Everywhere People Move into Darkness— Alleyways That Run Arms Between Them	5
It's Like There's Ash Everywhere	7
Undressing the Wound	8
The Only Brave People Are Medical Professionals	9
The Mind Is Hardwired for Narrative	10
Tsering Kyi	11
Examine the Vertebrae	12
He Undertook the Practice of Giving by Abandoning His Body	13
Waist Deep	14
Giving It Publicity Just Inspires Copycats	15
Everything I See Says Fire	16
Two Lines of Prayer	18
Malachi Ritscher	19
The Crowds Are Saying	20
Sita Enters the Fires of Vietnam	21
This Goes Beyond Turning the Other Cheek	22
The Helicopter Concerto Makes One Sound	23
People Who Soak Themselves in Petrol Are Not Martyrs	31

I Know Why My Father Says Spontaneous Combustion	32
We Were the Ones | Who Told Her to Write	33
Operators at Crematoriums Heat Corpses to 1,750 Degrees	34
He Tried Washing It From His Clothes	36
Zarmina	37
They Hold Their Prayer Beads in Their Right Hand— Every Tibetan Knows to Hold Them in Their Left	38
The Dalai Lama Will Not Speak	39
I Wouldn't Be Surprised if Most of These People Are Coerced	40
Conjuring	42
Announcement	44
There Were a Lot of Suicides That Year	45
Richard Pryor	46
Respect for Fire Is a Respect That's Been Taught	47
Gail Victorine	48
Here Is the Raw Material	49
Of Course, It's Not *Easy*	50
Secondhand	53
Sarah	54
The Image Combusting	55
Hu Jintao	56
Thousands Gather to Pray	57
The Body Underground Is the Same Reaction as Paper When It Burns	58
Notes	61
Charities	67
Acknowledgments	69

This is what my body teaches me: first of all, be wary of names; they are nothing but social tools, rigid concepts, little cages of meaning assigned, as you know, to keep us from getting mixed up with each other...

—Hélène Cixous

FLAMMABLE MATTER

: Set fire to yourself or don't. Either way, nobody will remember your cause twenty-four hours later. All they'll remember is thinking, *Strange that his hair didn't burn off first.*

: I think I can say with certainty: *Yes, the world is listening.*

Flammable Matter

I pluck their ripe names.
Hold them on my tongue til they redden.

How many fires can I fit in my mouth
before I burn, too?

Last week my father told me
      spontaneous combustion.

A body's bones can become
sets of stones rubbing against each other in sparks.

I didn't believe him.

Is this how reporters feel?

I don't know what a man on fire looks like
sprinting down the street or standing calmly

as his t-shirt melts with skin.

Richard Pryor once set himself ablaze
freebasing cocaine and drinking 151-proof rum.

Dressed in a bright red suit
in front of a microphone and an audience of thousands

he lit a match inches from his face
bounced it back and forth, and joked:

What's that? Richard Pryor running down the street.

Morocco

All I see is cheap horror flick:
the camera's shaky frame bordered by screams

until they burst—buckshot from the lens.
Streams of colored shirts

scattered men and women
who have struggled to find work. And there—

a wisp of light in the screen's corner.
An old garbage can set ablaze? No.

A man dancing through a six-foot flame
his head and limbs flailing against the authorities

who douse him in darkness. The camera cuts
to the man silhouetted by a white wall.

Shirtless and dazed, flanks of skin fall
from his face and body. Congealed blood

dangles in thin strips of leather as he raises his arm.
The crowd's muffled blare.

Sherab Tsedor

He put a statement on Facebook. Carried a Tibetan flag he forgot to wave. A lighter. Press releases. A bottle of paint thinner. There will always be scars, of course. He still has dressings on one leg. Not until the hospital. He doesn't remember shouting as they flew through him. The police know he has protested in Delhi's diplomatic quarter before. The Chinese embassy where he got off the bus. *I was sure he would understand.* His father, a refugee at four. *Sorry for all my mistakes.* He turned off his phone. *If only I lit more than my legs.* Had time to pour the thinner. Brothers and sisters burned awake with the world's attention. Because he is still alive it was a failure. *I've seen the news.*

Everywhere People Move into Darkness—
Alleyways That Run Arms Between Them

Bruno received a package including a will,
keys, and instructions on what should be done.

    All evidence pointed to the body being his friend.

He hasn't shown up, said Malachi's sister

    but police were still confirming dental records—
    his car found nearby.

Bruno began making calls:

    the jazz locals were certain
    it was the man best known for documenting

        Paul Rutherford, Gold Sparkle, Isotope 217:
        those were other people's bands.

Malachi was fiercely modest—
for at least the last decade he was an empty bottle

    with a familiar face.

An eyewitness said turning vehicles didn't stop
to watch a man become voltage on the highway.

    The *Sun-Times* once tried to do a piece
    but he declined

        saying he wanted to write his own obituary.

In Chicago, Malachi is not a crown or a halo

    but a small item set on fire
    during rush hour Friday morning.

It's Like There's Ash Everywhere

Not the way you think, but when you walk outside
you can feel its fingers tap your lungs.

My parents tell me they used the building
for triage, but it looks the same.

All the little old women wear surgical masks
in the street, and we wonder why

men with bleating wands
move mute throughout our classrooms.

I'm just happy to be back from Brooklyn.
Basketball season has started. Sometimes I cough

when we run suicides during practice.
No one talks about what happened

but I've heard some kids are in therapy
some kids saw the planes

and bodies
and think they're still falling.

Undressing the Wound

I stare into two Afghan burn victims:
one woman sits naked in the background

a black bar printed across her vagina
as if this is how shame comes to be

born of petrol and matchstick
camera lens and video clip

a step from the screen: women undressed
then dressed and undressed again

no more than fifteen or sixteen
married to men with shrapnel

in their teeth. Near bone thin
with bloodstained gauze

clinging to their breasts
unable to look away

: Set fire to yourself or don't. Either way, nobody will remember your cause twenty-four hours later. All they'll remember is thinking, *Strange that his hair didn't burn off first.*

: I think I can say with certainty: *Yes, the world is listening.*

: The only brave people are medical professionals who don't shout, *Moron*, and let the person die.

: I find it sad the only way for these people to receive attention is to take their lives in such a way.

The Mind Is Hardwired for Narrative

Even at five, Lobsang helped to gather the grazing flocks.

He was such a strong boy, said his mother.
Lobsang cared for more than his faith.

In the summer, they'd go swimming
when they'd finished tending their small farm.

Perfect for knifing through a hundred meters of still water
his long limbs hung as ornaments on his dark red robe.

On Tuesday, he stood still in the center
of the monastery, set himself alight

and marched through the open doors
toward the local government's office.

At his cremation ceremony
his mother holds the last photograph of her son

his hand propped against one high cheekbone
a pair of prayer beads overlapping his wrist.

When you tell someone a fact
they only consider if it is true, she says.

But not when you tell them a story.

Tsering Kyi

When I was young they told our parents, here is your plot. Then sent us to school in town. The government doesn't care if the herds dwindle, if we can pay for a ride to school. My father bought me books, and I held them close. There were no extra copies to go around. Just because we are nomads doesn't mean we lack a sense of home. I could hear the sirens echo all the way from the hills. As if they don't know what they're doing. All my best teachers were fired. It took only two tries for a station to sell petrol to me, a girl with no car. You can see the choices you're given if you wait long enough. They're the ones who bound the pastures in barbed wire, the ones who sent soldiers to our schools. What was I supposed to do? Everyone in the market just stood there and watched.

Examine the Vertebrae

Lift each name that floats beyond
its margins and tether it back to spine:
flint to gather, flint for two hands
to spark the breath. I collect their names,
dates of death, scraps of cloth soaked
in petrol that fail to light. Can two hands take
without intention? I write without permission—
miles and bodies mounting in fonts.
There are poets who question my ethics.
Monks who offer their brothers and sisters
before the headlines take them. A mother
still swears her daughter tripped
into the blaze. Women climb into clay ovens
and I wonder if there's ever been a choice.
A bodhisattva once thrust each limb
through amulets of fire to praise the Buddha.
As a child I learned to keep an arm's distance
to plunge my hand beneath cold water
if it brushed the flame. A Hindu prince
once had his wife walk a pyre to prove her faith.
When she emerged from the other side
not even the hem of her dress was burnt.

He Undertook the Practice of Giving
by Abandoning His Body

Here there were no hell-dwellers,
no hungry ghosts, and no calamities.

The land was the level palm of one hand
made of lapis lazuli

adorned with jeweled trees and flower-covered canopies
which all the bodhisattvas sat beneath during prayer.

One was devoted solely to worshipping the Buddha
and paid homage

with petals and powdered sandalwood
which he made fall from the sky.

But this is not equal to the offering of my body, he thought
covering his skin in fragrant oil.

And with no more than his vows
he set his body alight

illuminating as many worlds
as there are grains of sand along the Ganges.

All the buddhas of these worlds praised him, saying:
Son of a virtuous family, this is the supreme offering.

Waist Deep

Videos rarely show
the protest.

Fire and aftermath:

I hear *ash*
watch the spine's hollow wick catch

the flames of black bones

irises murky and
darkened with dense blood.

We never saw the earthquake

the landslide pinning
what could be branches

but are body parts of a family.

We talk ethics in class:
I show my students photographs

of a girl trapped waist deep in mud
her body sinking into flames

skin flaking and fluttering away
in ashy scales:

try not to breathe them in.

: Set fire to yourself or don't. Either way, nobody will remember your cause twenty-four hours later. All they'll remember is thinking, *Strange that his hair didn't burn off first.*

: I think I can say with certainty: *Yes, the world is listening.*

: The only brave people are medical professionals who don't shout, *Moron*, and let the person die.

: I find it sad the only way for these people to receive attention is to take their lives in such a way.

: Giving it publicity just inspires copycats. It's lost the impact of Thich Quang Duc. *Everybody* is doing it these days.

: Whatever your views on self-immolation, you can't help but be astonished at the otherworldly stance in that image, a monk amidst the flames on a Saigon street.

Everything I See Says Fire

When the self-proclaimed *dirty white kid*
begins talking to himself
                                      I change cars

and find him again as I peer up from my book

pleading for the rest of $18.50—
a bus ticket to his cousin's.

Yes, I'm writing this out of guilt
or the fear I still feel

as I offer a twenty with no questions:

the kid berating himself
more than his drunken dad

shaking *God* from his lips
and the contents from his backpack.

In class my teacher says
                            resting pose

but all I think is *Malachi*,

the boy's thumb conjuring flame from its cover,
a man stripping into a shadow of fire.

I read of young monks
whose families hold their final words again and again.

Do I write a warm hand on my own shoulder?

I close my eyes
and listen to her footsteps circle the room.

You are a fire-breathing dragon
my teacher says. *Relax*

> *let the muscle melt from bone.*

Two Lines of Prayer

Empathy is ninety-eight percent burns to the body
a handful of self-immolations

in grainy cell phone photographs and video
one man in flames

plastered along the narrow streets of New Delhi
a town adopted by Tibetan exiles.

When Tibet sings
it is a song of kindling bones

of Jamphel Yeshi written in gold
with thirty other names and thirty more.

Yeshi's name, a black poster
with bloody handprints put up days ago.

Monks, shopkeepers, and tourists stared.
A cousin visited him before his death

and mourned that Yeshi could not hear
in the early evening, two hundred monks marched

through the town center waving flags
and carrying banners that declared:

It was all over Facebook today
everyone was talking about it.

Malachi Ritscher

It's always the same debate between friends, colleagues, and comment boxes across the Internet: What is God? Some think He's Santa Claus, rewarding with presents and punishing with lumps of coal. But I know God as the Easter Bunny, hiding a video camera, a canister of gasoline, a sign: What has happened to my country? God does not choose. God does not make. God does not endorse. God does not smite. God does not sit on a cloud of prayers. He does not burn or weep or bear, but watches the bird drop even to its death. Am I therefore a martyr or a terrorist? a sign that reads, Thou Shalt Not Kill? or a video that has yet to be released by police more concerned with TV than a human body so badly charred it was impossible to determine its sex. Anyone can stand over the Kennedy Expressway just west of the downtown Loop. Maybe some will be scared enough to walk from their waking dream state to the base of a twenty-five foot sculpture: The Flame of the Millennium. I want the simplest form. Maybe you are less happy. Maybe not.

The Crowds Are Saying I am writing this because His name was Lobsang All the soldiers carry fire extinguishers She was still raising her hand Did they shout any slogans I was shopping when they ran down the street No one has been allowed to visit They wrapped themselves in barbed wire I have no claim to these lives It has been a waste of time I saw him swallow kerosene They couldn't put out the flames What can poetry do anyway He was nineteen years old The police threw the body in a truck Are you checking We were told they were being treated The Internet is closed All these patriots have been tortured Plainclothes police are everywhere Another white man appropriating pain Tell the world what is happening They don't understand The telephones are guarded I had to come The animal is anemic They only use his mouth

Sita Enters the Fires of Vietnam

After hearing these accusations
Sita became bowed with shame.

O son of Sumitra, prepare for me a pyre
the only remedy for this calamity.

Under the rule of Ngo Dinh Diem
South Vietnam favored

the country's Catholic minority
suppressing its Buddhist monks.

Agonized by these false rumors, I cannot bear living.
I shall enter a blazing fire, the only course left

now that I have been rejected in a public gathering.

After saying this, Sita sat
at a busy downtown intersection.

Two of her fellow monks poured gasoline over her
as a large crowd of Buddhists and reporters watched

her enter the blazing fire

her palms pressed in an arrowhead against her chest
her feet tracing a narrow path through the flames.

She burned while seated in the lotus position
the body slowly withering and shriveling up

the head blackened and charring.

: Set fire to yourself or don't. Either way, nobody will remember your cause twenty-four hours later. All they'll remember is thinking, *Strange that his hair didn't burn off first.*

    : I think I can say with certainty: *Yes, the world is listening.*

: The only brave people are medical professionals who don't shout, *Moron,* and let the person die.

    : I find it sad the only way for these people to receive attention is to take their lives in such a way.

: Giving it publicity just inspires copycats. It's lost the impact of Thich Quang Duc. *Everybody* is doing it these days.

    : Whatever your views on self-immolation, you can't help but be astonished at the otherworldly stance in that image, a monk amidst the flames on a Saigon street.

: This goes beyond turning the other cheek. It's public manipulation to create a sense of violence when the other side isn't willing to provide it.

    : History is filled with people who willfully court every sort of horrific death for an invisible principle. Martyrdom is hardly new. It's in the heart of many.

The Helicopter Concerto Makes One Sound

I. The Thing That Pisses Me Off Is They Never Ask Why

As I mentioned before
about changing minds

                                      To say something is stupid or ineffective
                                        is denigrating to the people who do it

The key is communication:
you have to look into their motivations

                                                    A lot is driven by culture

Most soldiers I know can't communicate

                                        It really comes down to sincerity

After a while they develop this kind of fear

                                             The guys who flew planes
                                           into the Towers were sincere

They mistrust another culture

                                             and so we despise them

II. People Have Spoken of the Monks Who Burned

In Saigon: a Buddhist parade with a hypnotic chant
robed priests marching

                                    When I was in school they showed it on TV

From the crowd came a frail old priest taking the lotus posture
and another priest pouring gasoline

                                    You'd see them covered and set on fire

Suddenly—towering flames

                                    The priests and nuns wailing
                                        toward this burning figure

And there he sat
unflinching to the smell of flesh and gasoline

                                    People here were horrified

It had enormous consequences

                                  I don't think it had political effect

inside Vietnam. It was so dramatic

                                        when it hit the headlines

all over the world. People thought

                                          it was a form of protest:

they saw the face of Buddha in the clouds that night

III. It's Meant to Go in One Eye and Out the Other

                                                  I was mostly on firebases
                                                    or out in the mountains

How did this man die?

                                              We were not going around
                                                  setting villages on fire

He threw grenades at the Marines

                                        I was in transit only a few times

Instead of just one, he threw three

                                                      I was not involved
                                                in community interaction

A Marine spotted him
and that's how he got it:

                                                contrary to popular belief

those two holes in his eye and throat
were done by sniper rifles

IV. Some of These People Come Back to Us

They live in the village between here
and the railroad to the west

          It's going to sound strange

We've had so much trouble moving through this area
a lot of civilians were killed as a result

        I had little interaction with Vietnamese

We found a few caves and blew them
picked up some weapons, shot a few V.C.

       There might be some mama-sans back on base

We just heli-lifted five suspects for interrogation
down at Hoi Yen or Dinh Banh

            They huddle real close

The mothers watch their children through the night

       There was also interaction with the chieu hoi

They know these people and get the idea
they know more than they're telling us

         Former Vietcong who switched sides

They go along riverbanks with us

         They look just like anybody else

but when they have a weapon, they're free game

V. The Demo Man Usually Blows It Up

How do you destroy this much rice?

                                              In Japanese culture you have seppuku
                         where you absolve the soul through disembowelment

Traditional Oriental patience makes them willing
to carry over the struggle from generation to generation

                         You can go back to World War II and the kamikazes:
                            Japanese pilots whose planes turned to bombs

In other words: equality and freedom

                             We would accuse the kamikazes of being insane
                                   they only had fuel to go in one direction

I wouldn't trade one dead American
for fifty dead Chinamen

                    Yet if you had a Marine jump on a grenade to protect his unit
                                                        he was a hero

VI. When You Measure or Weigh Anything You Change Its Nature

                Now you're almost getting into the debate about abortion

The prisoners were executed in our outfit as standard policy

                                  That may sound strange

We were taught in training how to take prisoners

                        That it's not an individual's right to take a life

Once we got to Vietnam it was an entirely different story

                      Which is the argument of the conscientious objector

They said, *You can't trust 'em. You know, slant-eyed. Those gooks are no good*

VII. My Position Is Times When There's Justification

                The critical issue is that they chose to attack civilians

They are such a magnificent group of fighting men

                I forget who it was but someone just got reamed
                saying the men who flew those planes were brave

They are the subject of our constant concern

                They struck what they felt they could strike

Their morale is extremely high

                That's what made it an act of terror

They always have a smile

                This was the only honorable way they could come up with

We sang three hymns and had a nice prayer
for the four men killed the other day

                You could say we've conducted drone attacks
                in Pakistan and civilians have been killed—

My feelings for America just soar when

                it can be written off as collateral damage

I turn around and look at their faces
determined and reverent at the same time

                If you want to know about war

                              my best advice isn't to go read

But still, they're a bloody good bunch of killers

                         We could go on investigating for hours

: Set fire to yourself or don't. Either way, nobody will remember your cause twenty-four hours later. All they'll remember is thinking, *Strange that his hair didn't burn off first.*

: I think I can say with certainty: *Yes, the world is listening.*

: The only brave people are medical professionals who don't shout, *Moron*, and let the person die.

: I find it sad the only way for these people to receive attention is to take their lives in such a way.

: Giving it publicity just inspires copycats. It's lost the impact of Thich Quang Duc. *Everybody* is doing it these days.

: Whatever your views on self-immolation, you can't help but be astonished at the otherworldly stance in that image, a monk amidst the flames on a Saigon street.

: This goes beyond turning the other cheek. It's public manipulation to create a sense of violence when the other side isn't willing to provide it.

: History is filled with people who willfully court every sort of horrific death for an invisible principle. Martyrdom is hardly new. It's in the heart of many.

: People who soak themselves in petrol are not martyrs. Martyrdom is suffering death because of your faith, not dousing it all over the headlines.

: It's difficult to comprehend the act of burning yourself to death, certainly in Western minds, but the very least we can do is try to understand why.

I Know Why My Father Says Spontaneous Combustion

A tiger steals through rows of oversized leaves.

I have never seen Vietnam beyond this screen.
A few scanned photographs. The black of my father's eyes.

These images tell nothing of a man burning far
past the dense green in his sight. Of my father

crouched in its belly, winding the overgrowth
with a box of metal strapped to his back

a radio receiver in hand. Too many gray plumes rise
and disperse to name the bodies below

in the street, a man becomes a torch midday
and all I can see is the white behind him.

We Were the Ones | Who Told Her to Write

    Zarmina's parents stand before a grave
                                  Amail lost her fiancé to a landmine last year
covered in loose gravel with no headstone
three women kneel over three smaller plots
                        in Pashtun tradition, she must marry one
                        of his two surviving brothers—against her will
        one murmurs Zarmina's name
                        like Amail, Zarmina is forbidden to leave her home
  It was an accident, whispers her mother
                        after she is caught reading
       Zarmina's father nods:
                        love poems over the phone
  She was a good girl, an uneducated girl
                        from childhood, she is engaged
                        to marry her first cousin
       He gathers her belongings
                        and the boy visits her home
a few books, scrawled-on pieces of paper
                        hoping to win her father's approval
   I don't know if he'll hide them
      or burn them, her aunt says
                      he refuses, knowing
                      he'll have to support the couple
        she was such a good poet,
Zarmina's 15-year-old neighbor confirms
                      weeks later, while cleaning the house
                      she locks the door—
she was trying to stay warm after her bath
  but the wood was wet with lighter fluid
                      by the time her mother reaches her
                      Zarmina is unrecognizable

Operators at Crematoriums Heat Corpses to 1,750 Degrees

When I was a kid, a boy at school burned his hand: the stench so thick and rich my tongue folded to the roof of my mouth. In Houston, a man burns the remains of his strangled girlfriend over his barbeque. Neighbors notice the acrid odor drifting across their lawns. As they smolder, organs often swell with gas. Firefighters call these bodies *bloaters*, say, *You'll know it when you smell one. You never get it out of your nose entirely, no matter how long you live.* In school, we light fabric swatches to test the smell. The ash and odor tell us what is burning. Cotton equals burnt leaves, its ash soft and white. Wool is like singed hair, its residue a dark, brittle bead that clings to my nostrils for days. When a whole body burns, it has a coppery, metallic odor from all the blood still inside.

He Tried Washing It From His Clothes

Mohammed had owned a vegetable stand
in Sidi Bouzid for seven years

when a policewoman confiscated his goods

spat in his face
and insulted his dead father.

He went to city headquarters to complain.
Never got past the doors.

An hour later he returned
to the building of arched shutters

and set himself ablaze.

He did not die, but lingered in a hospital bed

fumes of his flesh seeping through nurses' uniforms
and even the clothes of his guests.

There was so much anger
that President Ben Ali came to the foot of his bed.

Ten days after Mohammed died
the dictator's twenty-three year rule of Tunisia was over.

A few hundred feet from where he burned
hundreds of young men erect handwritten banners.

We are all people of sacrifice, reads one.

Not a single official has come, says Issawi Naja,
an unemployed teacher. *We need to clean the system.*

Mohammad Boukhari leans against a graffitied wall
and lights a cigarette.

I have a Ph.D. and work in a supermarket,
he says. *It smells of him.*

Zarmina

Because I am a girl, no one knows my birthday. At fifteen my father married me to an older man. To face him and his beatings or to burn when I tired of those. He knew I was in love with my cousin. I had been engaged to him for two years before my father decided money was more important than his daughter. I made it five years. My mother and sister came home and must have smelled the smoke. But I had locked the door behind me. They say I was trying to stay warm after my bath. That I slipped and caught my hem in the fire. Mother, you know I am not a clumsy girl. You have seen me dance, seen my poetry even before Father forced that, too, into the flames. I called my friend, Amail, from the hospital in Kandahar. Asked for her brother to come, impersonate a doctor from Kabul. I hear my parents bring reporters to my grave. That they ask about my poems. They don't deserve this much attention. I am just learning to write.

**They Hold Their Prayer Beads in Their Right Hand—
Every Tibetan Knows to Hold Them in Their Left**

Twenty thousand officials form dossiers for each monk
they "befriend." Plainclothes police who track their every step

describe self-immolators as outcasts and terrorists.
Chain the streets in their flak jackets. Surveillance cameras

hang from the eaves of temples. Last month
police raided a white-walled monastery in Gansu Province

kicked in the doors and smashed every computer. *They ran out
of handcuffs, so they tied our wrists with rope from the monastery.*

A million portraits of Mao Zedong hang on walls.
Photographs of the Dalai Lama burn.

A senior aide to Hu Jintao says
Temples have undergone a delightful change.

The Dalai Lama Will Not Speak

Boys and girls fill creases
of their robes with resistance

backs twisted white wicks
before the flames burn down

the camera's still
never bow to the brightness

but as the body's fabric
refuses to unwind

★

I send you flowers, their bright heads
huddled in a box on your doorstep

but go only once with you to Mass
and do not kneel or bow my head

in silence, but throw my eyes
to the brightness cast down

where I pick it up and place it
on my tongue

: Set fire to yourself or don't. Either way, nobody will remember your cause twenty-four hours later. All they'll remember is thinking, *Strange that his hair didn't burn off first.*

: I think I can say with certainty: *Yes, the world is listening.*

: The only brave people are medical professionals who don't shout, *Moron*, and let the person die.

: I find it sad the only way for these people to receive attention is to take their lives in such a way.

: Giving it publicity just inspires copycats. It's lost the impact of Thich Quang Duc. *Everybody* is doing it these days.

: Whatever your views on self-immolation, you can't help but be astonished at the otherworldly stance in that image, a monk amidst the flames on a Saigon street.

: This goes beyond turning the other cheek. It's public manipulation to create a sense of violence when the other side isn't willing to provide it.

: History is filled with people who willfully court every sort of horrific death for an invisible principle. Martyrdom is hardly new. It's in the heart of many.

: People who soak themselves in petrol are not martyrs. Martyrdom is suffering death because of your faith, not dousing it all over the headlines.

: It's difficult to comprehend the act of burning yourself to death, certainly in Western minds, but the very least we can do is try to understand why.

: I wouldn't be surprised if most of these people are coerced and the rest are just desperately lonely.

: It takes deep introspection to conclude their actions deserve that final commitment. Such are the judgments these men and women make.

Conjuring

The last image of Kyi is a five-liter can of fuel.

Hours after confiscating cell phones
and threatening witnesses

Chinese security blamed *separatist plots*
and said Kyi suffered from depression.

Tibetans say the self-immolations
are born from what remains.

It's not so hard to pray, said Kyi.
Even in the summer pastures

a small tent sheltered a sculpture of the Buddha
and a picture of the Dalai Lama.

When Kyi returned to Machu in the fall
the streets crowded with her classmates.

A new government policy
bound the high pastures with barbed wire.

Police cars and government buildings burned
into the morning as students watched

cupping small candles from the wind.

Hundreds were detained
but they would not go home.

Kyi entered a public toilet
discarded her traditional Tibetan overdress

and doused herself in petrol.

She walked out into the vegetable market
and became a report of another burning.

Announcement

In recent days, four self-immolations instigated by separatist powers, from both inside and outside the Dalai Clique, happened in the prefecture. It has influenced the harmony and stability of society, and impacted the people's joyful living and working.

Self-immolation is an extremist suicide action, which means anti-human, anti-society, and anti-law. It deprives the human being of the right of life. This sort of terrorist action not only wastes the love and care given by parents and society, but also demises or tramples one's own life. It is an action completely irresponsible for family and society. Recent self-immolations in our prefecture are the political conspiracy of the Dalai Clique's attempts to separate China, and to destroy the unity of nationalities.

The public must recognize the situation, and make a clear distinction between right and wrong, cherish your lives, and be active in fighting this criminal action. To accurately dig out the evil backstage manipulator in a timely manner, to strike hard against the criminal action that violates the law, to safeguard the harmony and stability of the prefecture with the utmost effort, Gan-nan Tibetan Autonomous Prefecture Public Security Bureau has made the decision shown below.

1. Amount of RMB 50,000 will be awarded to anyone who reports and provides the police reliable clues related to planning, instigating, manipulating, and luring for self-immolation.

2. Amount of RMB 200,000 will be awarded to anyone who accurately reveals the evil backstage manipulator for the four recent self-immolations.

3. Police will completely keep the identity confidential, and ensure the security of the informant.

4. The award will be given through a special path and process.

Informant's hot-line telephone:
Landline: 0941-66962710941-6696272
Cellular: 1529366901115293669012
Gan-nan Prefecture Public Security Bureau

There Were a Lot of Suicides That Year

Academic Magnet and School of the Arts students
gather near the parking spot of Aaron Williams

as a boom box he was known for plays.

The father of the high school student
who set himself on fire near the front entrance this week

says his son *was struck with despair so deep he could not see.*

Trace Williams appeared briefly before news media
to explain his son's death. Reading a prepared statement

and citing a note written by the 16-year-old
Williams said the suicide was meant

to emphasize the importance of living life with compassion.
Even in the midst of despair, his thoughtful nature came through.

The complete letter was not made available
but Williams said his son *was suddenly confused*

when a 17-year-old from a nearby school
was found hanging in his bedroom closet.

Jason Sakran of the Charleston County School District
says the students at Academic Magnet

spent most of Friday listening to music
and consoling one another.

They were trying to be as normal as possible.

Richard Pryor

You live around white people in this country and anything can happen. I'm talking a year later I'm drawn up fucked up and out of my mind. I never thought I'd rise through a loophole of fire in a skin streaming with light. He had too much to live for, that's what they said. You find God quick when they find your ass dead. Fire is inspirational. They should use it in the Olympics. I did the hundred-yard dash in 4.3. I didn't have anything else, figured I might as well have some sun on my face. You don't feel shit for three days til your nerves wake up. Most people say you've been punished by God. Pipe would say, come on in the room, Rich. It took me three times to catch. They said I burnt fifty percent of my body. He had given me all this and what did I do with it? Maybe I did have a heart attack screwing one of the most attractive white women ever, shoot up my wife's car when she tried to leave. On stage, I had more humanity than a Sunday school teacher. Who else spun gold from such a scarred life? They said I died on June 9, 1980. It's hard enough just being a human being.

Respect for Fire Is a Respect That's Been Taught

A man heads toward the hollow of a crowd.

He sacrificed himself, said Moshe's sister
after giving doctors permission

to remove the tubes feeding life
into what's left of her brother.

Sixty miles from his mother and father
Moshe Silman is ninety-four percent burns

a tower of flames reaching
toward what we can only name.

We underestimate the need
to understand through touch.

He arrived in Tel Aviv Saturday night
with gasoline and a suicide note:

*The state of Israel stole from me and left me
with nothing. I will not be homeless.*

We are peaceful anarchists, said Ofir Avigad,
a leader of last year's protests

and founding member
of a newly opened bar and restaurant.

*We have humor. People have a limit
to how much ideology they want with their beer.*

Gail Victorine

Every time I hear the song I think of the boy. I was about eight. We were coming out of synagogue. It must have been the High Holy Days. A little boy my age had been playing with matches and died in a house fire. "Night and Day" was on the radio. In Englewood, there was a black part of town, and I experienced this sadness: that this type of thing would never happen to me, because I was white and privileged. I so often felt this way. Why was this little boy alone? Why did he have access to matches? I never discussed this with my parents. I've never discussed this with anyone. Rosh Hashanah is such a happy time of year. Such a pretty time of year. Why was he alone? Why didn't someone protect him? How could he be by himself? Funny the things that shake you.

Here Is the Raw Material

Are they dead yet?
    And rising.
  This is where the words break
or do they borrow—steal?

How many voices stretch
  drummed skin over my own?

  Afghan women with surnames
    of flame.
Tibetan monks blazing
  beyond their bright orange robes.

  There are boys burning.
There will be more tomorrow.

How many do I know
  past glass and glass?

How many lines must I stitch
    to form a single face
    a breath
  and body beyond its frame?

  Rob the grave / raise the dead
watch breast melt to bone.

This is how the towers fall
  a hundred blocks away
  in a hundred million homes.

Some of us watch the ash
            and walk away.

    Some of us have to go back.

: The only brave people are medical professionals who don't shout, *A toron*, and let the person die.

: I find it sad the only way for these people to receive attention is to take their lives in such a way.

: Giving it publicity just inspires copycats. It's lost the impact of Thich Quang Duc. *Everybody* is doing it these days.

: Whatever your views on self-immolation, you can't help but be astonished at the otherworldly stance in that image, a monk amidst the flames on a Saigon street.

: This goes beyond turning the other cheek. It's public manipulation to create a sense of violence when the other side isn't willing to provide it.

: History is filled with people who willfully court every sort of horrific death for an invisible principle. Martyrdom is hardly new. It's in the heart of many.

: People who soak themselves in petrol are not martyrs. Martyrdom is suffering death because of your faith, not dousing it all over the headlines.

: It's difficult to comprehend the act of burning yourself to death, certainly in Western minds, but the very least we can do is try to understand why.

: I wouldn't be surprised if most of these people are coerced and the rest are just desperately lonely.

: It takes deep introspection to conclude their actions deserve that final commitment. Such are the judgments these men and women make.

: Of course, it's not *easy*. Jumping from the ledge of a skyscraper is not *easy*. Flying into the World Trade Center is not *easy*.

: These comments just show how little we believe in any cause, and how inseparable we've become from the couch.

Secondhand

the burning is too far away
to glimpse more than smoke:

luck is just another word for *distance*
pressing my face flush to glass

of a TV screen instead of the window
of my Tribeca high school

bodies plummet hundreds of stories
a single body smolders to a charring less than bone

men and women throb in thick waves of limbs
hoping for so much real when they cannot touch it

I walk through museums of marble stands
two months later when I return

all my walls are intact
my fire comes contained

Sarah

I remember it happening in the spring. But when I looked it up it was December. I was mentoring a girls group at a high school, but it didn't happen there. My girls were so upset. I don't remember there being any news coverage. I guess they try not to cover things like that. There was a magnet high school right next to an art school. One day this person I remember being a girl set herself on fire between the two, so students from both schools could watch. I didn't realize they were so close, enough that they locked both down. They didn't cancel class though. They dismissed at the regular time.

★

The story I read said it was a boy. And the headline read something like, He Was Trying to Harm Himself. I thought that was obvious. He doused his clothes in lighter fluid, lit them on fire, and walked to the main entrance. A bunch of kids saw and texted their parents to come because they were terrified. I wonder did they take any pictures. People from the school grabbed fire extinguishers and threw a blanket over him until the cops came and took him to a hospital in Georgia where he died. They kept on posting updates as the story developed.

★

I remember why I thought it was a girl. Because, initially, they thought it was a girl. It reminds me of Malachi: a body too badly charred to determine its sex. Although he was still alive when they flew him to Georgia. Maybe I'm just imagining a second person. There were a lot of suicides that year. I just know that person was on fire.

The Image Combusting

We talk movies as we ride north.

    That one Miranda July film
        (I always forget its name):

John Hawkes sprints across his front lawn
        stops in front of his sons' bedroom window
            and sets his hand aflame.

        His wife watching as he heaps himself into boxes.
I watch the scene at least ten times.

I've told Josh I want my next project to be on Buchenwald.

    He's worried—knows my past
        is an unlit flame.

Says, *Why don't you write about basketball for a while.*

    I want to tell Josh: *These men and women are not depressed.*
Look at how they burn, mouths unspooling.

    You need to balance yourself out, he says.

        A match, when struck without purpose
            merely immolates itself.

    Why do we say *distance* but mean *fire*?
Say *fire* but mean *love*, filling with ash?

A body of third degree burns, I think
    sitting in my therapist's office

        reaching for what has already left.

Hu Jintao

Hours and hours of research, documents you don't understand: I began in scrap metals and then moved on. Six months from now you'll be looking for blades that swing and swing. When my father was a merchant I never slept soundly, and there never was a day to tap a man's pain. I have seen books that talk. If this situation sounds too familiar, let's zoom in. Imagine the richest campfire at your throat. Millions in Tibet. It's not going to stop.

Thousands Gather to Pray

Yet again they burn: translated words left behind,
last notes for friends and family.

Authorities recruit monks for firefighting teams
turning temple prayer halls into fire stations.

The Chinese Communist Party's 18th National Congress
marks more than ninety Tibetan self-immolations.

The ten-year leadership transition follows the announcement:
Anyone inciting self-immolation will be charged with murder.

A forty-year-old monk and his nephew are arrested in Sichuan
for sending photographs of protesters to India as eight people burn.

The Foreign Ministry says the issue has nothing to do
with human rights, ethnicity, or religion.

Lorong Konchok says he was following orders of the Dalai Lama.
The Tibetan government-in-exile says his statement was coerced.

The Body Underground Is the Same Reaction as Paper When It Burns

This is the artist cutting limb from limb
        burning in the dark.

For a few months I was obsessed with September 11th.

      All those people who consciously chose
to burn in the buildings, says James.

When we place a body in the earth
                we remember where.

      My mother still lights candles for her parents
          each year on their birthdays.

I light one for my Aunt Jill days after she dies
        watch it flicker on Sarah's night stand.

              I don't make it to her funeral.

Instead, I am here, in Chicago
        drawing faces from ash.

      I am scared of planes crashing.
          Of not making it from New York.

What is guilt but the distance between?

      My brother says I should be there.
          I can't take my cousin, Debra, crying on the phone.

There are tribes who refuse the camera's eye
    journalists who only peer through it.

        Fire is more than light captured.

Tell me I am making a map.
    Tell me I will know how to read it when I'm done.

Notes

My hope is for these poems to open a space for empathy, and to honor the voices of the men, women, and children who have self-immolated—not to steal from them. If nothing else, they seek to give life to those who are no longer here.

Portions of these poems are inspired by or adapted/appropriated from the following sources:

Set Fire to Yourself or Don't
Comment Field Responses. Olsen, Alexa. "Tibetans Self-Immolate Outside Lhasa Temple." *The Huffington Post.* The Huffington Post, 28 May 2012.

Flammable Matter
Richard Pryor Live on the Sunset Strip. Dir. Joy Layton. Perf. Richard Pryor. Warner Bros., 1982.

Morocco
Fev, Amal. "فيديو حلظة إحتراق الأطر العليا بالرباط." *YouTube.* YouTube, 18 Jan. 2012.

Goodman, David J. "Self-Immolation Protest in Morocco Captured on Video." *The Lede: Blogging the News with Robert Mackey.* The New York Times, 19 Jan. 2012.

"Moroccans Burn Selves in Unemployment Protest." *Al Jazeera English.* Al Jazeera, 20 Jan. 2012.

Sherab Tsedor
Burke, Jason. "Protesters' Stories: Sherab Tsedor and Tibet." *The Guardian.* Guardian News and Media, 13 Jan. 2012.

Everywhere People Move into Darkness—Alleyways That Run Arms Between Them
"Malachi Ritscher: Out of Time." *Savage Sound: Gallery 100.* Savage Sound Syndicate, 2006.

Margasak, Peter. "Malachi Ritscher's Apparent Suicide." *Chicago Reader.* Chicago Reader, 7 Nov. 2006.

Undressing the Wound
Qureshi, Ahmad. "Graph of Self-Immolation among Afghan Women Shows Rise in Herat." *Rawa News.* Rawa News, 30 Aug. 2008.

The Only Brave People Are Medical Professionals
Comment Field Responses. Olsen, Alexa. "Tibetans Self-Immolate Outside Lhasa Temple." *The Huffington Post.* The Huffington Post, 28 May 2012.

The Mind Is Hardwired for Narrative
Park, Madison. "Teenage Monk Self-Immolates in China." *CNN*. Cable News Network, 18 July 2012.

"Tibetans Continue to Set Themselves on Fire." *Free Tibet*. Free Tibet, 17 July 2012.

Tsering Kyi
Burke, Jason. "One Tibetan Woman's Tragic Path to Self-Immolation." *The Guardian*. Guardian News and Media, 26 Mar. 2012.

Holding, Dane. "Both a Teenage Schoolgirl and a Mother of Four Self-Immolate in Protest." *The Tibet Post International*. The Tibet Post International, 05 Mar. 2012.

Examine the Vertebrae
Rajagopalachari, C., and Vālmīki. *Ramayana*. Mumbai, India: P.V. Sankarankutty Dy. Registrar for the Bharatiya Vidya Bhavan, 2006.

He Undertook the Practice of Giving by Abandoning His Body
The Lotus Sutra: Taishō Volume 9, Number 262. Trans. Tsugunari Kubo and Akira Yuyama. Berkley: Bukkyō Dendō Kyōkai and Numata Center for Buddhist Translation and Research, 2007.

Waist Deep
McQuade, Donald, and Christine McQuade. "Pair: Frank Fournier, Omayra Sanchez, Colombia, 1985 [photograph] and Isabel Allende, Omayra Sanchez [essay]." *Seeing & Writing 4*. Boston: Bedford/St. Martin's, 2010. 590-92.

Giving It Publicity Just Inspires Copycats
Comment Field Responses. Olsen, Alexa. "Tibetans Self-Immolate Outside Lhasa Temple." *The Huffington Post*. The Huffington Post, 28 May 2012.

Two Lines of Prayer
"Pawo Jamphel Yeshi Passes Away." *Tibetan Youth Congress*. Tibetan Youth Congress, 28 Mar. 2012.

"Tibetan Protester Dies after Setting Himself on Fire in New Delhi." *MI News 26*. Freelancer Television Broadcasting, 28 Mar. 2012.

Wong, Edward. "Tibetan Exiles Rally Around Delhi Self-Immolator." *The New York Times*. The New York Times, 29 Mar. 2012.

Malachi Ritscher
Abebe, Nitsuh. "Malachi Ritscher, 1954-2006." *Pitchfork*. Pitchfork Media Inc., 14 Nov. 2006.

Ritscher, Malachi. "Malachi Ritscher, Iraq War Casualty: Mission Statement." *YouTube*. YouTube, 26 July 2007.

Ritscher, Malachi. "Mission Statement." *Savage Sound: Gallery 99*. Savage Sound Syndicate, 2006.

Weaver, Matthew. "The Quiet Death of Malachi Ritscher." *The Guardian*. Guardian News and Media, 29 July 2006.

The Crowds Are Saying
Lloyd-Roberts, Sue. "Self-Immolations Shake Tibetan Resolve." *BBC News*. BBC, 18 Apr. 2012.

Sita Enters the Fires of Vietnam
"Ramayana—Chapter 116: Sita's Trial by Fire." *YouSigma.com*. YouSigma.com, n.d.

Sanburn, Josh. "A Brief History of Self-Immolation." *Time: World*. Time, 20 Jan. 2011.

"'The Ramayana'—Full Text Translation by Romesh C. Dutt, Book 12." *About.com—Religion and Spirituality: Hinduism*. About.com, n.d.

"The Self-Immolation of Thich Quang Duc." *Buddhism Today*. Buddhism Today, 7 Jan. 2000.

This Goes Beyond Turning the Other Cheek
Comment Field Responses. Olsen, Alexa. "Tibetans Self-Immolate Outside Lhasa Temple." *The Huffington Post*. The Huffington Post, 28 May 2012.

The Helicopter Concerto Makes One Sound
In the Year of the Pig. Dir. Emile De Antonio. Perf. Harry S. Ashmore and Daniel Berrigan. Homevision, 1968.

Victorine, James. Personal Interview. 3 Nov. 2012.

People Who Soak Themselves in Petrol Are Not Martyrs
Comment Field Responses. Olsen, Alexa. "Tibetans Self-Immolate Outside Lhasa Temple." *The Huffington Post*. The Huffington Post, 28 May 2012.

We Were the Ones | Who Told Her to Write
Griswold, Eliza. "Why Afghan Women Risk Death to Write Poetry." *The New York Times*. The New York Times, 29 Apr. 2012.

Operators at Crematoriums Heat Corpses to 1,750 Degrees
Tsai, Michelle. "What's the Smell of Burning Human Flesh?" *Slate Magazine*. The Slate Group, a Division of the Washington Post Company, 26 Mar. 2007.

"The Fire Test to Differentiate Fabrics." *Dharma Trading Co*. Dharma Trading Co., n.d.

"What Does Burning Flesh Smell Like?" *Yahoo! Answers*. Yahoo!, 2011.

He Tried Washing It From His Clothes
Abouzeid, Rania. "Bouazizi: The Man Who Set Himself and Tunisia on Fire." *Time*. Time, 21 Jan. 2011.

Zarmina
Griswold, Eliza. "Why Afghan Women Risk Death to Write Poetry." *The New York Times*. The New York Times, 29 Apr. 2012.

They Hold Their Prayer Beads in Their Right Hand—
Every Tibetan Knows to Hold Them in Their Left
Jacobs, Andrew. "Tibetan Self-Immolations Rise as China Tightens Grip." *The New York Times*. The New York Times, 22 Mar. 2012.

I Wouldn't Be Surprised if Most of These People Are Coerced
Comment Field Responses. Olsen, Alexa. "Tibetans Self-Immolate Outside Lhasa Temple." *The Huffington Post*. The Huffington Post, 28 May 2012.

Conjuring
Burke, Jason. "One Tibetan Woman's Tragic Path to Self-Immolation." *The Guardian*. Guardian News and Media, 26 Mar. 2012.

Holding, Dane. "Both a Teenage Schoolgirl and a Mother of Four Self-Immolate in Protest." *The Tibet Post International*. The Tibet Post International, 05 Mar. 2012.

Announcement
"Chinese Authorities Offer Large Rewards for Information on 'Black Hand' Behind Tibetan Self-Immolations." *International Campaign for Tibet*. International Campaign for Tibet, 24 Oct. 2012.

Craggs, Ryan. "China Self-Immolations: Police Offer Cash For Tips On Immolators." *The Huffington Post*. The Huffington Post, 25 Oct. 2012.

There Were a Lot of Suicides That Year
Parker, Adam. "Father: My son 'was struck by a despair so deep that he could not see beyond it.'" *The Post and Courier*. Evening Post Publishing Co., 11 Dec. 2010.

Richard Pryor
Richard Pryor Live on the Sunset Strip. Dir. Joy Layton. Perf. Richard Pryor. Warner Bros., 1982.

Upton, Julian. "Extinguishing Features: The Last Years of Richard Pryor." *Bright Lights Film Journal*. Bright Lights Film Journal, May 2007.

Respect for Fire Is a Respect That's Been Taught
Bachelard, Gaston. *The Psychoanalysis of Fire*. Trans. Alan C. M. Ross Boston: Beacon Press, 1968. Print.

Reporting., Isabel Kershner; Dina Kraft Contributed. "Israeli's Act of Despair Disheartens a Movement." *The New York Times.* The New York Times, 17 July 2012.

Rudoren, Jodi. "Israel: Protester Dies After Self-Immolation." *The New York Times.* The New York Times, 21 July 2012.

Gail Victorine
Hirsch, Gail. Personal Interview. 5 October. 2012.

Of Course, It's Not *Easy*
Comment Field Responses. Olsen, Alexa. "Tibetans Self-Immolate Outside Lhasa Temple." *The Huffington Post.* The Huffington Post, 28 May 2012.

Sarah
Tarkany, Sarah. Personal Interview. 18 February. 2013.

The Image Combusting
Me and You and Everyone We Know. Dir. Miranda July. Perf. John Hawkes, Miranda July, Miles Thompson, Brandon Ratcliff and Charlie Westerman. IFC Films. 2005.

Hu Jintao
(Horse_ebooks). Twitter Feed, 26 Aug.-26 Sep. 2012.

Thousands Gather to Pray
Banyan. "Self-Immolation in Tibet: The Burning Issue." *The Economist*. The Economist Newspaper, 9 Dec. 2012.

"China Protests U.S. Comments on Tibet, Says 'Disgusting'" *NBC News*. NBC News, 7 Dec. 2012.

"Storm in the Grasslands: Self-Immolations in Tibet and Chinese Policy." International Campaign for Tibet. Washington, DC, 2012.

The Body Underground Is the Same Reaction as Paper When It Burns
Ali, Kazim. *The Disappearance of Seth*. 1st. Wilkes-Barr: Etruscan Press, 2009.

Charities

Below are a few of the many worthwhile charities that work to resolve some of the myriad of social and political injustices that are explored within *Flammable Matter*. Please consider donating your time and/or resources to one or more of them.

Help the Afghan Children
3900 Jermantown Road, Suite 300
Fairfax, VA 22033
(703) 848-0407
info@htac.org
www.helptheafghanchildren.org

International Campaign for Tibet
1825 Jefferson Place NW
Washington, DC 20036 USA
(202) 785-1515
info@savetibet.org
www.savetibet.org

Project RENEW
Kids First Village
185 Ly Thuong Kiet Street
Dong Ha City, Quang Tri Province, Viet Nam
+84 53 3858445 (ext. 114)
projectrenewvietnam@gmail.com
landmines.org.vn

Women for Women International
Global Headquarters
2000 M Street, NW
Suite 200
Washington DC 20036
(202) 737-7705
general@womenforwomen.org
www.womenforwomen.org

Acknowledgments

I would like to thank the editors of these publications in which previous versions of the following poems first appeared:

Columbia Poetry Review, "Flammable Matter" and "Richard Pryor"
DIALOGIST, "Respect for Fire Is a Respect That's Been Taught"
PANK, "Waist Deep"
Phantom Books, "Everywhere People Move into Darkness—Alleyways That Run Arms Between Them"
The Bakery, "Conjuring" and "I Know Why My Father Says Spontaneous Combustion"
Vinyl Poetry, "It's Like There's Ash Everywhere"

Thank you to Tony Trigilio for inspiring the manuscript and guiding me through the process of its creation, and to Dana Curtis of Elixir Press for believing in it enough to put it out in the world. Gratitude to all the supportive current and former faculty and staff at Columbia College Chicago: Jenny Boully, CM Burroughs, Lisa Fishman, Jill Magi, Michael Robins, David Trinidad, and Nicole Wilson. Thank you to my peers at Columbia College Chicago, who without, these poems would not be possible, especially those who helped workshop previous incarnations of this manuscript: Joshua Young, m. forajter, Brian Miles, Tara Boswell, Patrick Samuel, Andrew Ruzkowski, Jordan Hill, and Kate Magnolia Glasgow.

Gratitude to my parents, Gail Hirsch and Jim Victorine, and to Sarah Tarkany, for their constant love and support, and for their generosity in giving their voices to some of these poems. Thank you again to Sarah for being my constant editor and poetry sage.

Love and thanks to the rest of my family, especially Joe and Liz Victorine.

Thank you to Stevie Edwards and the rest of the staff at *Muzzle* who have given me space to discuss poems and hone my craft through my reviews.

Shout out to Theo Angus for shooting my author photo and to Noah Zagor and MEYVN for lending us space and time.

Last but not least, thank you to the slam and spoken word communities in New York, New Jersey, and Chicago that have offered a respite through performance, and thank you to the people from these communities who have helped push me to get here, especially: Rock Wilk, Jahnìlli AKA, Ocean Vuong, Justin Woo, Thomas Fucaloro, Marty McConnell, and Emily Rose Kahn-Sheahan.

JACOB VICTORINE was born and raised in New York City. He earned his MFA in Poetry from Columbia College Chicago, where he teaches a class on performance poetry. His poems appear in places such as *Columbia Poetry Review, Vinyl Poetry, Matter, DIALOGIST, Phantom Books,* and *PANK,* which nominated him for a Pushcart Prize in 2013. He has published essays in *Publishers Weekly* and *Poets Quarterly* and serves as a Book Reviewer for *Publishers Weekly* and *Muzzle Magazine*. As a competitive slam poet, he has twice been a Grand Slam Finalist at the Mental Graffiti slam in Chicago and was a member of the 2011 Jersey City National Poetry Slam Team. He currently lives in Chicago with his girlfriend and their cat, Gilgamesh. *Flammable Matter* is his first book.

TITLES FROM ELIXIR PRESS

Poetry

Circassian Girl by Michelle Mitchell-Foust
Imago Mundi by Michelle Mitchell-Foust
Distance From Birth by Tracy Philpot
Original White Animals by Tracy Philpot
Flow Blue by Sarah Kennedy
A Witch's Dictionary by Sarah Kennedy
The Gold Thread by Sarah Kennedy
Rapture by Sarah Kennedy
Monster Zero by Jay Snodgrass
Drag by Duriel E. Harris
Running the Voodoo Down by Jim McGarrah
Assignation at Vanishing Point by Jane Satterfield
Her Familiars by Jane Satterfield
The Jewish Fake Book by Sima Rabinowitz
Recital by Samn Stockwell
Murder Ballads by Jake Adam York
Floating Girl (Angel of War) by Robert Randolph
Puritan Spectacle by Robert Strong
X-testaments by Karen Zealand
Keeping the Tigers Behind Us by Glenn J. Freeman
Bonneville by Jenny Mueller
Cities of Flesh and the Dead by Diann Blakely
Green Ink Wings by Sherre Myers
Orange Reminds You Of Listening by Kristin Abraham
In What I Have Done & What I Have Failed To Do by Joseph P. Wood
Bray by Paul Gibbons
The Halo Rule by Teresa Leo
Perpetual Care by Katie Cappello
The Raindrop's Gospel: The Trials of St. Jerome and St. Paula by Maurya Simon
Prelude to Air from Water by Sandy Florian
Let Me Open You A Swan by Deborah Bogen
Cargo by Kristin Kelly
Spit by Esther Lee
Rag & Bone by Kathrym Nuernberger
Kingdom of Throat-stuck Luck by George Kalamaras
Mormon Boy by S. Brady Tucker
Nostalgia for the Criminal Past by Kathleen Winter
Little Oblivion by Susan Allspaw
Quelled Communiqués by Chloe Joan Lopez
Stupor by David Ray Vance
Curio by John Nieves
The Rub by Ariana-Sophia Kartsonis
Visiting Indira Gandhi's Palmist by Kirun Kapur
Freaked by Liz Robbins
Looming by Jennifer Franklin
Flammable Matter by Jacob Victorine
Prayer Book for the Anxious by Josephine Yu
flicker by Lisa Bickmore

Fiction

How Things Break by Kerala Goodkin
Juju by Judy Moffat
Grass by Sean Aden Lovelace
Hymn of Ash by George Looney
Nine Ten Again by Phil Condon
Memory Sickness by Phong Nguyen
Troglodyte by Tracy DeBrincat
The Loss of All Lost Things by Amina Gautier